The Samaritan

JEFFREY HOLTAN

WestBow
PRESS®
A DIVISION OF THOMAS NELSON
& ZONDERVAN

Scriptures taken from the Holy Bible, New International Version®, NIV®.
Copyright © 1973, 1978, 1984, 2011 by Biblica, Inc.™ Used by permission
of Zondervan. All rights reserved worldwide. www.zondervan.com The
"NIV" and "New International Version" are trademarks registered in
the United States Patent and Trademark Office by Biblica, Inc.™

WestBow Press books may be ordered through booksellers or by contacting:

WestBow Press
A Division of Thomas Nelson & Zondervan
1663 Liberty Drive
Bloomington, IN 47403
www.westbowpress.com
1 (866) 928-1240

Because of the dynamic nature of the Internet, any web addresses or
links contained in this book may have changed since publication and
may no longer be valid. The views expressed in this work are solely those
of the author and do not necessarily reflect the views of the publisher,
and the publisher hereby disclaims any responsibility for them.

Any people depicted in stock imagery provided by Thinkstock are
models, and such images are being used for illustrative purposes only.
Certain stock imagery © Thinkstock.

ISBN: 978-1-5127-6626-4 (sc)
ISBN: 978-1-5127-6627-1 (e)

Library of Congress Control Number: 2016919617

Print information available on the last page.

WestBow Press rev. date: 11/30/2016

This book is dedicated to Jesus Christ
who loves me from eternity
and to my wife, Deb, who loves me every day.

ACKNOWLEDGEMENTS

I T IS ONLY BY the grace of God that I write these words. God, in his grace, used a number of Christian brothers and sisters to call me out of the darkness of despair to the light of forgiveness. The following brothers and sisters in Christ served me as instruments of God's grace: Mary Holtan, Daniel Deutschlander, Richard Phillipsen, Kris Eggers, Virginia Cartwright, Darrell Roecker, and Robert Holtan. I also thank my children, Abigail, Magdalene, and Caleb, for sharing the gift of forgiveness with me. A special thanks to these agents of grace!

PREFACE

A S I STRUGGLED THROUGH a time of horrible guilt, I looked for something to help me along the way. I found a few people who helped me tremendously. I found a number of Bible passages that filled me with comfort when I needed it. I found a few passages in some books that grabbed my attention. I found a few hymn stanzas that soothed my soul. What I did not find was a resource directed to my struggle with guilt. So, with the help of God and the encouragement of my family, I decided to share my experience with the world. If you or someone you know is suffering from guilt over a sin or sins they have committed, this book is meant to speak to you or your friend. I don't profess to have all the answers. However, I offer the one answer that helps the most – Jesus Christ. Please give this short work a read. Consider it a travel guide through the challenging journey of guilt. I pray this account helps you to know the forgiveness that is yours in Christ.

A WARNING WORD
TO THE WISE

Pride goes before destruction, a haughty spirit before a fall.
—Proverbs 16:18

"I WOULD NEVER DO THAT! No matter what happens, I will remain faithful!" Have similar words passed over your lips? We can be so self-assured. We can be so bold and certain. We think that we can single-handedly take on Satan and his allies. But friends, consider life apart from the delusion of sinful pride. Peter and his cohorts were convinced beyond any doubt that they would boldly stand with Jesus, even to the point of death. They were quite certain they would not even consider fleeing from him to save themselves. Even after Jesus warned Peter, "Truly, I tell you, this very night before the rooster crows twice, you will deny me three times," Peter still insisted, "If I must die with you, I will not deny you." All the other disciples said the same thing. But how did this really turn out? Peter ended up saying, "I don't know this man of whom you speak." As those words left his mouth, the rooster crowed for the second time. "And Peter remembered how Jesus had said to him, 'Before the rooster crows twice, you will deny me three times!' And he broke down and wept."[1] Pride preceded the fall. The fall brought Peter to tears. Please note the pattern.

Allow one more word of warning. This one comes from the life of King David. David exhibited a firm trust in the Lord from youth. David was the Lord's anointed—a man after the Lord's own heart. David was faithful. He weathered the hard times with a focus on God's promises. He handled wealth and fame with a humble thankfulness—until one spring day. "In the spring, at the time when kings go off to war, David sent Joab out with the King's men and the whole Israelite army. They destroyed the Ammonites and besieged Rahab. But David remained in Jerusalem" (2 Samuel 11:1). David did not lead his troops to battle. Perhaps his pride led him to think he could afford to take some time off. However, his idleness got him into trouble. Adultery led to a cover-up. The lies started. The cover-up led to murder. Sin ruled the day. Guilt began to destroy David from the inside. And then for months, guilt tormented him.

> When I kept silent, my bones wasted away through my groaning all day long. For day and night your hand was heavy upon me; my strength was sapped as in the heat of summer. (Psalm 32:3–4)

> I am worn out from groaning; all night long I flood my bed with weeping and drench my couch with tears. My eyes grow weak with sorrow; they fail because of all my foes. (Psalm 6:6–7)

> My guilt has overwhelmed me like a burden too heavy to bear. (Psalm 38:4)

> So my spirit grows faint within me; my heart within me is dismayed. (Psalm 143:4)

Finally, the prophet Nathan visited David. It was time to face his sin. David listened to a story that illustrated the depth of his sin. David heard Nathan proclaim, "You are the man!" David confessed his sin and heard the sweet words of absolution: "The Lord has taken away your sin. You are not going to die." Forgiveness is free. Forgiveness sends the guilt packing, and it relieves the heartache. However, even forgiven sin comes with consequences. So Nathan said, "But because by doing this you have shown utter contempt for the Lord, the son born to you will die" (2 Samuel 12:14).

So you see that sin is no respecter of persons. It can ruin you as it ruined Peter and David. There is only one way to overcome sin: trust in Jesus, who defeated sin for us. A humble trust is what God gives us. Don't foolishly try to fight Satan and sin on your own. You will fail. Put your trust in Jesus. Look to him alone for deliverance from sin and guilt. Please take Paul's warning to heart! "So if you think you are standing firm, be careful that you don't fall!" (1 Corinthians 10:12).

For our struggle is not against flesh and blood,
but against the rulers, against the authorities, against
the powers of this dark world and against the
spiritual forces of evil in the heavenly realms.
—Ephesians 6:12

THE SIN

I PROMISED TO FAITHFULLY FOLLOW Jesus at my confirmation. I promised to remain faithful to my wife in my marriage vows. I promised to watch my life and doctrine closely at my ordination as a Christian pastor. I failed at all of that. After years of faithful service as a Lutheran pastor, I ruined it all with the sin of adultery.

Scripture is quite clear in its directions to husbands. Clearly I failed to live by God's law. Hebrews 13:4 says, "Marriage should be honored by all, and the marriage bed kept pure, for God will judge the adulterer and all the sexually immoral." Scripture is equally clear in God's requirements for leaders in the church. Paul wrote to Timothy, "Now the overseer must be above reproach." So what happened?

It started out with a woman I was counseling who made it clear that she was attracted to me. At that point I referred her to another counselor and was determined to avoid her at all costs. I failed. I did not flee from sin. In pride, I thought I could handle it on my own. I couldn't. I slid right down the slippery slope into a sexual relationship. Not only did I sin sexually, but I also became an accomplished liar. I lied to myself, my wife, my children, my congregations, and church leaders. All this sin weighed me down. Even before my sin was discovered, I sat at my desk in the church office praying to God, "Lord, I am broken. Please fix me!" The rest of this story will show how God answered that prayer.

So many times God gave me opportunities to confess my sin. So many times I lied. Finally, the Lord made it so I couldn't lie anymore. I had to say what I did. It was a beautiful June morning, sunny with blue skies—yet it was the worst morning of my life. (Spiritually speaking, it was a good day to start the process of unburdening my soul.) That morning I walked through the door of the parsonage to the demand to tell my wife what I had done.

"Say it! Say what you have done!"

Those words were echoed by my oldest daughter, who was determined to keep me away from my family. Those words still haunt me. I began to see how my sin had destroyed the biggest blessings in my life. So after all the lies, the confession came: "I had sex with her!"

So the demand to leave came from my wife and was again echoed by my oldest child as the other two were waking up and were trying to figure out what was happening. "Get out!" Those were the final words as the door shut behind me. I left, walked over to the church office, and resigned from the ministry, never to return. I moved out of the parsonage. I moved in with my mother. That was the first of many difficult conversations telling people who loved me about my sin. The guilt began to consume me. I tried to relieve the guilt by looking for a job. The Lord used this job hunt to destroy any remaining pride in my heart. At the same time, the guilt increased. I did not sleep. When I finally did sleep, the dreams began. It was always Satan accusing me. He would not stop reminding me of my sin. The dreams grew more frequent and more vivid. The one nightmare that repeated over and over again was Satan kneeling on my chest, looking me in the eyes, and whispering in my ear, "Your soul is mine! Welcome to hell, preacher!" I had nothing. No job. No money. No wife. No family. Even opening the Bible to read was a chore. Going to church was a struggle. Nothing was joyful; everything was dark.

My thinking was clouded by guilt. All seemed lost. I began to think that it didn't matter how I lived anymore. So I saw her again. Then I lied about it over and over. Things kept getting worse. But the Lord never gave up on me. In some ways I had given up on me. Many people had given up. It appeared to me that my family despised me and that my wife hated me. The reality is that they were hurt deeply by my sinful actions. The reality is also that they loved me every day.

A part-time job came along, and then a full-time job. I worked as much as I could. I tried my best to support my children. Yet everything remained in complete shambles. I talked to Deb occasionally, mostly about the children. I was always happy to talk to her, but I would be sad by the end of the conversation. Abby, our oldest, would not talk to me. Maggie wanted very little to do with me. Caleb was just angry. So I worked two jobs, slept very little, and lived in guilt. That guilt was turning into shame. I began to see myself in everything as a complete failure with no future. Counseling helped to a point. But I only felt better for an hour or so. Most of the counseling focused on making sure I was not suicidal. I guess that was important, but I never felt very comforted. My sin was still eating away at me.

At this time I found myself not able to make it through a workday without crying. I missed my family. I missed the ministry. I despised myself and my sinful decisions. I felt the Lord's hand heavy upon me. I knew he forgave me in Christ. But my family had not forgiven me. More than that, I had not forgiven myself. I felt like such a fool. I deserved nothing but hatred from everyone. In the end all this was my fault! I was guilty!

Day after day I felt the weight of my sin. I would think about how I had destroyed life for Deb and the children. I would think of how I had brought a bad name to Christ, his church, and the office of the ministry. It was all just too much. While I was not suicidal, I did want to die.

By October something started to change little by little. Just as I started to accept the fact that not only would ministry not be my career, but my marriage would end also, something started happening very slowly. Deb had been praying for me. She had been begging people to reach out to me. Some people did reach out to me and just at the right time.

I began to seek help again. This time I thought of a former college professor. God would use him to help me. The difference was in his approach to the matter. He began with a message from God's law. Like Nathan saying to David, "You are the man!" Oh, what a relief! No more tiptoeing around the problem. "You have sinned!" Yes, I had. No disagreeing from me. Then it was time to move on to the gospel. So I was finally on my way out of the pit of despair. It was back to the baptismal font. I am a child of God! I am forgiven! My guilt is gone through the blood of Christ. Consequences for my sin would continue, but the guilt had no power anymore. (Of course, guilt still comes and goes, but at this point I could feel the chokehold of guilt weakening.)

Counseling sessions came and went. Visits with the children happened occasionally. The holidays approached. Visits with Deb came and went. As my healing continued in these beginning stages, I decided I would write an apology or a confession of my sin. So I wrote the following:

My story is a shameful story. At this point I feel the deepest remorse and guilt. I feel dirty, ashamed, embarrassed, and disgusted with myself. I have become the very thing I never wanted to become. I have ruined many lives, lost many friendships, hurt the ones I loved most, and above all sinned against God. I have broken the sixth commandment. More than that, I have lied to my family.

The law of God continues to press me hard. Satan continues to accuse me day after day. Guilt is tormenting me. There is the guilt of how I have sinned against God. There is guilt over how I have destroyed God's gift of marriage. There is guilt over how I have hurt my children. There is guilt over the sadness I have brought God's people. There is a deep sadness in my heart over losing the privilege of serving in the public ministry.

For seventeen years I had the greatest privilege in the world to publicly proclaim the gospel to God's people. It is indeed the greatest privilege in the world! I thank God every day for this great privilege. I was indeed a faithful soldier doing daily battle with the devil and his evil angels. In the midst of the daily grind, I lost my focus on Christ. I became a mere professional. I let down my guard and acted foolishly. My actions led to my current condition. I have been wounded in battle. The devil won the victory in the battle. I am injured to the point that I will not return to the battle, at least not in the same capacity. I find myself hurting inside. The guilt is overwhelming. I now know by experience the words of the psalmist, "For day and night your hand was heavy upon me; my strength was sapped as in the heat of summer." I would have never believed how much guilt could plague a person. The attacks of Satan are relentless. He keeps on throwing my sin in my face. Oh, how I long for the past! Oh, how I regret my foolish decisions. I wish I had never sinned.

I cannot undo the past. While I lost the battle, Christ won the war! What sweet news! What incredible joy! I am forgiven! I cannot hear that sweet, good news enough! Oh, how I love the words of absolution! Oh, what great joy to receive the body and blood of Christ! I am forgiven! Christ became sin for me. He became what he loathed for the likes of me! I am a baptized child of God!

I am humbled. I struggle with guilt. I am forgiven. I pray every day for the strength to live according to God's Word. I pray every day for God to send someone into my life to assure me and remind me of the forgiveness Christ has won for me! Would you please help me, pray for me, and remind me of Christ's forgiveness?

There were a few reactions to this confession. Many people were happy to see it. Some were compelled to contact me with incredible gospel comfort. Others said nothing. Still others criticized the confession as too focused on me and not focused enough on Christ. I certainly understand the criticism. However, this was not a confession of my faith. It was a confession of my sin. Christ alone was the answer to my sin and my guilt. God used all of this for my spiritual good.

As improvement came for me spiritually, it came as a slow, painful struggle—one step forward, two back. I was not always truthful. I lied about an attempted contact with my adultery partner. It was about a phone call. It was a phone call in which I told her I did not want to speak with her anymore. I did not want to talk about what happened, and I tried to hide the whole conversation. After this incident, it seemed as if my marriage would end. The divorce was scheduled for March, and it was January. But God intervened again! My lie and my feeble attempt at a cover up demonstrated that I could not fix anything. Only God's grace could bring good from all the bad in me and around me. After a phone conversation with Deb, in which she told me she wanted nothing more to do with me, I gave up. While I gave up, God did not. With another visit to my former college professor and his intervention, Deb changed her mind. We began counseling together shortly after this. At this time I contacted a friend to help me. I gave him access to my phone records, e-mails, bank account, and credit card. He agreed to handle any contacts from the gal with whom I had the affair. He also agreed to pray for me and support me as I sought to recover from my sin and reunite with my family.

Slowly and steadily, through much work, many prayers, and more tears, things began to change for the better. On March 10, 2012, we renewed our marriage vows. God is good! However, the work continued. We continued our marriage counseling. We were also blessed to attend a marriage retreat for couples who were in turmoil because of unfaithfulness. This came about because of a book entitled *Unfaithful.*[2] So in February of 2013, almost a year after we renewed our vows, we attended the Hope and Healing[3] retreat. This was a very difficult and emotional weekend. However, we benefitted greatly from a weekend in which we were forced to deal with things we tended to avoid. In addition, it was good to be with people who were experiencing the same pain. We left encouraged. We continue to work together to improve our relationship.

I truly hope that the reader understands that while this was a time of increased happiness for me and my family, it was not a walk in the park. Trust had to be restored a little at a time. Church was a welcomed help each week, but we couldn't make it through a service without crying. Guilt continues to haunt me at times. So this means a daily return to baptism—daily contrition and repentance. Daily remembering that Jesus forgave me. Daily recalling that the flesh is weak. I cannot defeat the devil, the world, and my sinful self. It means daily growing in grace, feeding the trust in Jesus. The good news is that I don't have to defeat the unholy three—Jesus has!

> You who think of sin but lightly
> Nor suppose the evil great
> Here may view its nature rightly,
> Here its guilt may estimate.
> Mark the sacrifice appointed;
> See who bears the awful load;
> It's the Word, the Lord's Anointed,
> Son of Man and Son of God.[4]

WHY THE SAMARITAN?

I N JESUS' DAY SAMARITANS were outcasts. They were considered half-breeds by the Israelites. People looked down on them to say the least. Jesus had this in mind when he spoke of Samaritans in his teaching. In the three Samaritan accounts that we consider next, we will observe how Jesus used the plight and social standing of the Samaritans to teach people his unconditional gospel. Jesus came for all people—even those who are despised by others. My sin caused others to look down on me. My sin caused me to despise myself. I believe that these Samaritan accounts are very helpful to those of us who have struggled with guilt.

Guilt turns into shame. Shame is guilt on steroids. In guilt I feel sorry for what I have done. Guilt makes me feel devastated and embarrassed over my sinful actions. Guilt causes me to kick myself over a horrible decision. So often, even daily, I wish I had made a better decision. As guilt ate away at me, it became shame. Shame made me feel as if I could never again make a good decision, never do the right thing. We will observe a Samaritan woman who was filled with shame. We will notice how Jesus changed things for her.

Jesus does the same for us as we struggle with guilt and shame. We will learn of the depth of Jesus's love for us as we consider the Samaritan.

I hear the Savior say,
Thy strength indeed is small!
Child of weakness, watch and pray,
Find in Me thine all in all.

Jesus paid it all
All to Him I owe
Sin had left a crimson stain
He washed it white as snow.

Where—by Thy grace to claim
I'll wash my garments white
In the blood of Calvary's Lamb.[5]

WHAT IS THIS REALLY ALL ABOUT?

LOOK INTO THE PASTOR'S study. See me sitting there praying. Listen to me say, "Lord, I am broken. Please fix me." That is what this is all about. It is about God's grace. You have seen that God is at work fixing me, forgiving me, healing me. This is meant to help others who are praying a similar prayer.

If you have no sin to be forgiven, no guilt that troubles you, no shame over your sinful desires and deeds, no feelings of failure before God, then don't bother reading any more. Instead, spend some time reviewing the Ten Commandments and searching your soul for your sins and shortcomings before God. After that, come back for the help offered here. For those who are struggling with sin, guilt, and shame, listen carefully to the words of your gracious God!

This is all about God's love for sinners. He loves you enough to point out your sin! He loves you enough to discipline you. He loves you enough to give you consequences for your sins so you do not go back to them. He loves you enough to daily kill your sinful nature and bring a new person of faith to life. In love God reaches out to you through his word of truth, both law and gospel. He points out your sin, leads you to repent, and announces his loving forgiveness. Jesus came to seek and save the lost. Jesus came to call sinners to repentance. Jesus came to save people from their sins. So, dear reader, know your sins and repent of them! You are forgiven! As our dear Lord puts it, "Take heart, son; your sins are forgiven" (Matthew 9:2).

> I said, "I will confess my transgressions to the Lord"—and you forgave the guilt of my sin. (Psalm 32:5)

John 4

Now Jesus learned that the Pharisees had heard that he was gaining and baptizing more disciples than John—although in fact it was not Jesus who baptized, but his disciples. So he left Judea and went back once more to Galilee. Now he had to go through Samaria. So he came to a town in Samaria called Sychar, near the plot of ground Jacob had given to his son Joseph. Jacob's well was there, and Jesus, tired as he was from the journey, sat down by the well. It was about noon. When a Samaritan woman came to draw water, Jesus said to her, "Will you give me a drink?" (His disciples had gone into the town to buy food.) The Samaritan woman said to him, "You are a Jew and I am a Samaritan woman. How can you ask me for a drink?" (For Jews do not associate with Samaritans.) Jesus answered her, "If you knew the gift of God and who it is that asks you for a drink, you would have asked him and he would have given you living water." "Sir," the woman said, "you have nothing to draw with and the well is deep. Where can you get this living water? Are you greater than our father Jacob, who gave us the well and drank from it himself, as did also his sons and his livestock?" Jesus answered, "Everyone who drinks this water will be thirsty again, but whoever drinks the water I give them will never thirst. Indeed, the water I give them will become in them a spring of water welling up to eternal life." The woman said to him, "Sir, give me this water so that I won't get thirsty and have to keep coming here to draw water." He told her, "Go, call your husband and come back." "I have no husband," she replied. Jesus said to her, "You are right when you say you have no husband. The fact is, you have had five husbands, and the man you now have is not your husband. What you have just said is quite true." "Sir," the woman said, "I can see that you are a prophet. Our ancestors worshiped on this mountain, but you Jews claim that the place where we must worship is in Jerusalem." "Woman," Jesus replied, "believe me, a time is coming when you will worship the Father neither on this mountain nor in Jerusalem. You Samaritans worship what you do not know; we worship what we do know, for salvation is from the Jews. Yet a time is coming and has now come when the true worshipers will worship the Father in the Spirit and in truth, for they are the kind of worshipers the Father seeks. God is spirit, and his worshipers must worship in the Spirit and in truth." The woman said, "I know that Messiah" (called Christ) "is coming. When he comes, he will explain everything to us." Then Jesus declared, "I, the one speaking to you—I am he." Just then his disciples returned and were surprised to find him talking with a woman. But no one asked, "What do you want?" or "Why are you talking with her?" Then, leaving her water jar, the woman went back to the town and said to the people, "Come, see a man who told me everything I ever did. Could this be the Messiah?" They came out of the town and made their way toward him. Meanwhile his disciples urged him, "Rabbi, eat something." But he said to them, "I have food to eat that you know nothing about." Then his disciples said to each other, "Could someone have brought him food?" "My food," said Jesus, "is to do the will of him who sent me and to finish his work. Don't you have a saying, 'It's still four months until harvest'? I tell you, open your eyes and look at the fields! They are ripe for harvest. Even now the one who reaps draws a wage and harvests a crop for eternal life, so that the sower and the reaper may be glad together. Thus the saying 'One sows and another reaps' is true. I sent you to reap what you have not worked for. Others have done the hard work, and you have reaped the benefits of their labor." Many of the Samaritans from that town believed in him because of the woman's testimony, "He told me everything I ever did." So when the Samaritans came to him, they urged him to stay with them, and he stayed two days. And because of his words many more became believers. They said to the woman, "We no longer believe just because of what you said; now we have heard for ourselves, and we know that this man really is the Savior of the world." (John 4)

It was high noon at Jacob's Well, outside the town of Sychar. Jesus stopped to take a rest. At the same time, a woman from the village came out to get some water. The showdown was about to begin. This confrontation began in a very benign way. Jesus certainly needed some rest from traveling, and after such exertion, he needed some water. The Samaritan woman was trying to get some water also. But why was she getting water at high noon? Usually the women would get water in the morning and in the evening. It was wiser to do this important chore when it was a little cooler, not in the hot sun of high noon. Those who are struggling with sin and guilt understand why she would make her way for water at noon. She wanted to be alone. She did not want to see the dirty looks. She most definitely did not want anyone to talk to her about her sin. She did not want to talk about her failures. So she set out for water when she was sure no one else would be at the well. I so vividly recall avoiding people because I did not want to talk about my sin. At the same time, I felt bad because no one talked to me. I wanted to avoid the dirty looks, the whispers, the gossip, and even the innocent inquiries of how I was doing. I wanted nothing to do with those who looked down their noses in judgment. I was ashamed of what I had done and who I was. So I avoided people. This, of course, did nothing to help me.

Imagine the Samaritan woman's surprise when she found a man at the well! Now what? Should she leave and come back later? She did not recognize the man, so she continued on to the well. Perhaps he would not even speak to her. For this Samaritan woman, there was no getting around the very conversation she did not want to have.

Jesus paid no attention to the social reasons to avoid a conversation with this Samaritan woman. The custom of the day would not allow Jesus to speak with a woman, especially a Samaritan. In addition, this woman had a very bad reputation. Jesus did not allow these barriers to stop him from confronting her sin. Love was the motivating factor for Jesus. In love for this lost soul, he began the conversation. He started with a single request. He asked for her help. He got the drink of water he needed. She got the water she came for. But Jesus offered so much more! The conversation began with talk of "living water." This was talk about the promised Savior who came to quench the sinner's thirst for God. Jesus held out the promise of eternal life to this sin-sick soul. He called on her to receive the comfort only the Messiah could give.

The Samaritan woman was very interested in all this talk of living water. She wanted to avoid the hassle of coming to get water from the well. She was only beginning to understand what Jesus was really talking about. The conversation seemed easy enough, but now came the uncomfortable, personal part.

"Go get your husband." A simple request indeed. Except this simple request was the Samaritan's biggest fear. You can almost hear the woman thinking, *Oh here we go again! More judgmental preaching.* Jesus pointed out this woman's adulterous lifestyle. To her credit, she did nothing to hide her sin. She made no excuses. She did not blame others. In her own unique way, she admitted her guilt. "I have no husband ..."

The woman's guilty conscience compelled her to change the subject. Why would she want to dwell on such negative things? She started to talk about true worship. This gave Jesus the opportunity to share the gospel. She wanted to discuss the proper place of worship. Jesus showed her that the place was not important. He spoke about the object of worship instead of the place. Ultimately, true worship is focused on the Messiah. "I, the one speaking to you—I am he."

What an amazing impact Jesus's words had on this guilt-ridden woman! Her focus shifted from her own guilt to the one who takes guilt away. She was no longer concerned about covering up, hiding, and shifting attention away from her sin. She knew her sin. She also knew her Savior. So, touched by these loving words of eternal wisdom, she left her water behind and ran back to the village to share this incredible news. "Come, see a man who told me everything I ever did. Could this be the Messiah?"

All from a conversation with a sinful woman, an entire village came to know Jesus as the Savior of all. So, fellow guilty sinners, think about how God will use you. First, always remember that Jesus has forgiven you! Second, consider the struggle you have had with guilt. You have seen the dirty looks, heard the gossiping whispers, felt the sting of the judgmental words, and lost your pride. This makes you the ideal candidate to share the gospel, like this Samaritan woman. You are the Samaritan. In joy tell your village about the Savior!

> Therefore, there is now no condemnation for those who are in Christ Jesus! (Romans 8:1)

Luke 10:25–37

> On one occasion an expert in the law stood up to test Jesus. "Teacher," he asked, "what must I do to inherit eternal life?" "What is written in the Law?" he replied. "How do you read it?" He answered: "'Love the Lord your God with all your heart and with all your soul and with all your strength and with all your mind'; and, 'Love your neighbor as yourself.'" "You have answered correctly," Jesus replied. "Do this and you will live." But he wanted to justify himself,

so he asked Jesus, "And who is my neighbor?" In reply Jesus said: "A man was going down from Jerusalem to Jericho, when he fell into the hands of robbers. They stripped him of his clothes, beat him and went away, leaving him half dead. A priest happened to be going down the same road, and when he saw the man, he passed by on the other side. So too, a Levite, when he came to the place and saw him, passed by on the other side. But a Samaritan, as he traveled, came where the man was; and when he saw him, he took pity on him. He went to him and bandaged his wounds, pouring on oil and wine. Then he put the man on his own donkey, took him to an inn and took care of him. The next day he took out two silver coins and gave them to the innkeeper. 'Look after him,' he said, 'and when I return, I will reimburse you for any extra expense you may have.' "Which of these three do you think was a neighbor to the man who fell into the hands of robbers?" The expert in the law replied, "The one who had mercy on him." Jesus told him, "Go and do likewise." (Luke 10:25–37)

Here we see pride in action. The lawyer put Jesus to the test with the most important question of all. However, this man was confident in himself. He was sure he had met the requirements to enter eternal life. His focus was to show his debating skill. He was not focused on the eternal fate of his soul. So Jesus told this pointed story of the Good Samaritan.

Love is the fulfillment of the law. Love is a verb. Keep these two truths in mind as you read the account of the Good Samaritan. The lawyer trying to test Jesus thought he had this down. After all, he answered Jesus with a perfect summary of the law. But knowledge and action don't always go together. So Jesus made clear in his story. So Jesus drove it home with the simple statement, "Go and do likewise." In other words, show mercy to people in need. Put love into action.

We all must confess that we have failed to do this perfectly or even consistently. Those who recognize their sin and struggle with guilt will confess their lack of love for others. My sin of adultery was an unloving action on so many levels. It was my own realization of how unlovingly I had acted that made me suffer so. In the midst of a struggle with guilt, it is very easy to become jaded. Guilty people become bitter people. Guilty people start feeling sorry for themselves. The guilty become focused on how others have wronged them or failed to forgive them. This attitude stands in the way of showing love to others.

In the end I was like this teacher of the law. I knew the answers. I knew what God said. I failed to carry it out. How often we all fail! Perhaps your failure is different from my failure. Maybe your guilt is different from my guilt. But we are similar in that we have failed and feel guilty. We cannot justify ourselves. The man in this story tried and failed. Which brings us back to Jesus's parable.

As you read this account, see yourself as the traveler. You are the man left for dead. You are the helpless person in need of the Good Samaritan. Jesus is our Good Samaritan. He took pity on us even as we were his enemies. He gave up his life for us while we were still sinners. As Paul puts it, "But God demonstrates his own love for us in this: While we were still sinners, Christ died for us. Since we have been justified by his blood, how much more shall we be saved from God's wrath through him!" (Romans 5:8–9). Jesus rescued us from sin and guilt. He continues to care for us through his word of grace. He continues to strengthen us through the promise of holy baptism. He has put his name on us through water and the word. He promises to continue to love us unconditionally and forgive us. Jesus continues to strengthen us through his holy supper in which he gives us his body and blood for the forgiveness of our sins. Jesus is our Good Samaritan.

In realizing what Jesus has done for us, we rejoice. We are also moved to show love to those in need around us. Our dear Lord Jesus has lavished us with his rich mercy and amazing grace. It is his love and mercy that motivate us to help our neighbor. We love Jesus because he loved us first. Now we want to show our love for others. Yes, we want to be like this Good Samaritan. We want to love our neighbor. We want to forgive our neighbor. We want to serve our neighbor. All this is because Christ loves, forgives, and serves us.

It all sounds so simple. Christ loves—so we love. Christ forgives— so we forgive. Christ serves—so we serve. But this is where our struggle begins. We know what is right. Part of us wants to do what is right. But part of us (our sinful nature) wants to avoid this altogether. Yes, part of us wants to walk by on the other side of the road and not get involved. This is often where guilt will take hold of us once again. The devil loves to use guilt to trip us up and get us to fall back into our sinful ways. We begin to think to ourselves that we are not good enough to love, to forgive, or to serve. We can't do it. So we won't do it. In this way we fail. We prove ourselves to be sinners. We show our deep need for the Good Samaritan, Jesus. Jesus died and rose again! This means our many sins are paid for in full! You are forgiven! I am forgiven! We need to be reminded of this every day. It chases our guilt away. It strengthens us in our struggle. It turns us into good Samaritans, who seek to help and to serve those in need.

Martin Luther summarizes: "But Christ, the true Samaritan, takes the poor man to himself as his own, goes to him and does not require the helpless one to come to him for here is no merit, but pure grace and mercy; and he binds up his wounds, cares for him and pours in oil and wine, this is the whole gospel from beginning to end."[6]

The lawyer in this account came to Jesus to prove he was good enough for God. He thought he had secured himself a place in heaven. Jesus masterfully tells this story that summarizes spiritual truth. The truth of the matter is that none of us is the perfect neighbor. We do not fulfill the law because of our lack of love. Yet, Jesus in his perfect love for us fulfilled the law perfectly in our place. As we are connected to Jesus by faith, we are perfect in God's eyes, for when he sees us, he sees Jesus, the perfect Samaritan. Since we know Jesus loves us, we want to share his love with everyone around us.

What calling remains for the guilty sinner? This calling to be a neighbor! In repenting of sin and receiving God's forgiveness, we are restored to live a new life. What better way to say thank you to our Savior than to show love and give assistance to those in need?

Jesus teaches us that those who have been forgiven much, love much. This fact is illustrated in Luke 7:36–50:

> Now one of the Pharisees invited Jesus to have dinner with him, so he went to the Pharisee's house and reclined at the table. When a woman who had lived a sinful life in that town learned that Jesus was eating at the Pharisee's house, she brought an alabaster jar of perfume, and as she stood behind him at his feet weeping, she began to wet his feet with her tears. Then she wiped them

with her hair, kissed them and poured perfume on them. When the Pharisee who had invited him saw this, he said to himself, 'If this man were a prophet, he would know who is touching him and what kind of a woman she is – that she is a sinner.' Jesus answered him, 'Simon, I have something to tell you.' 'Tell me, teacher,' he said. 'Two men owed money to a certain moneylender. One owed him five hundred denarii, and the other fifty. Neither of them had the money to pay him back, so he canceled the debts of both. Now which of them will love him more?' Simon replied, 'I suppose the one who had the bigger debt canceled.' 'You have judged correctly,' Jesus said. Then he turned toward the woman and said to Simon, 'Do you see this woman? I came into your house. You did not give me any water for my feet, but she wet my feet with her tears and wiped them with her hair. You did not give me a kiss, but this woman, from the time I entered, has not stopped kissing my feet. You did not put oil on my head, but she has poured perfume on my feet. Therefore, I tell you, her many sins have been forgiven – for she loved much. But he who has been forgiven little loves little.' Then Jesus said to her, 'Your sins are forgiven.' The other guests began to say among themselves, 'Who is this who even forgives sins?' Jesus said to the woman, 'Your faith has saved you; go in peace."

A result of forgiveness is a deep love for the one who has forgiven. We have a deep love for Jesus because he has forgiven us. So we go in peace to share that love with the world!

This is love: not that we loved God, but that he
loved us and sent his Son as an atoning sacrifice for
our sins. Dear friends, since God so loved us, we
also ought to love one another. (1 John 4:10–11)

Luke 17:11–19

Now on his way to Jerusalem, Jesus traveled
along the border between Samaria and Galilee.
As he was going into a village, ten men who had
leprosy met him. They stood at a distance and
called out in a loud voice, "Jesus, Master, have
pity on us!" When he saw them, he said, "Go,
show yourselves to the priests." And as they went,
they were cleansed. One of them, when he saw
he was healed, came back, praising God in a loud
voice. He threw himself at Jesus' feet and thanked
him – and he was a Samaritan. Jesus asked, "Were
not all ten cleansed? Where are the other nine?
Was no one found to return and give praise to
God except this foreigner?" Then he said to him,
"Rise and go; your faith has made you well."
(Luke 17:11–19)

The cry went out, "Jesus, Master, have pity on us!" For centuries
God's people have echoed this cry in worship. The church has
sung, "Lord, have mercy on us! Christ, have mercy on us! Lord,
have mercy on us!" This is indeed an important request. We are
all beggars before God. Our only help is in this Lord of mercy.
These ten lepers needed the mercy Jesus alone could give. Jesus
said the word, and they were healed. We all have our own story
of a time of tragedy or trouble. At such times we cry out to Jesus
to have mercy on us. In his own way and in the deepest love for
us, he always shows us mercy. Above all he is the one who has

won our forgiveness. For all that our merciful Master has done, we are indeed thankful! But how thankful are we?

It is so easy, as this account illustrates, to receive what we asked for and go on with life. That is what nine of these lepers did. They were indeed healed. They were happy of course. They may have even had a passing thought of thankfulness. But they just kept on going. They were off to show themselves to the priests. They were eager to return to a normal life with their families and friends. Oh yes, they appreciated the gift of healing. Where they faltered was in becoming more enamored with the gift of healing than with the Healer. What we observe in the Samaritan in this account is that even before he shows himself to the priests, he returns to thank Jesus!

We strive for this same kind of top-of-the-mind thankfulness that takes hold of our hearts and lives. We do not want to focus solely on the gifts but more so on the Giver of the gifts. What's the difference? One man focused his thankful attention on Jesus, while the other nine focused their thankful attention on what Jesus had given them. This is no small difference! It is the difference between a passing feeling of thankfulness that remains silent and a thankfulness that remains top of the mind every day. How can we demonstrate this same kind of thankfulness in our lives?

We find the answer in this account of the thankful Samaritan. The least likely one of the ten to return in thankfulness is the only one who returns in thankfulness. This just underscores the fact that the gospel changes people.

It is easy for Christians to begin to take their faith for granted. After years of hearing the greatest news of all that our sins are forgiven in Christ, it can seem like a boring old story. Sometimes we even forget the power the gospel has. Once while dealing with a Christian family as their spiritual shepherd, I heard this attitude put into words. They were expressing some concern about a teacher in the congregation's school. As I attempted to defend the teacher and to share with them a plan put into place to help the teacher grow professionally, the couple dismissed it all as a plan that would never work. One of them said quite bluntly, "People can't change!" Thank God that this is not true! God changes people through the gospel. Look at the change Jesus made in the life of this Samaritan! Consider how God has changed you!

I vividly recall the changes that took place in my life. In committing the sin of adultery, I was moving away from God. Even as God mercifully called me back, Satan accused me, so I suffered through a period of great guilt. All I could muster was that simple cry, "Lord, have mercy on me!" Jesus graciously heard my cry. Through his gospel he comforted me, forgave me, changed me, and filled my heart with thankfulness.

Daily God's mercy extends to the unworthy, including you and me. Daily the Lord Jesus comes to us with his merciful forgiveness. His gospel brings change and healing. What a powerful invitation to thankful service! Jesus has taken your sin away. The spiritual disease that eats away at your heart is healed in his word of forgiveness. You stand before God clothed in Christ's perfection. Never take this life-changing truth for granted!

Nihil citius senescit quam gratia! "Nothing ages more quickly than gratitude!" Those ancient words still ring true! The sinful nature enjoys complaining, finding fault, criticizing others but not self, and making excuses for a lack of thankfulness. The sinful nature loathes thankfulness. For those of us who suffer from times of guilt, thankfulness is a huge challenge. So how do we remain thankful? How do we hold on to the top-of-mind thankfulness of the Samaritan? The gospel! Focus on the Giver! Know that he gives what we can never earn or deserve. Know that he loves you unconditionally. The more we dig into holy scripture, the more we are convinced of these facts and the more thankful we become. Our Lord Jesus has rescued us from our own sin. He has reconciled us to God. His actions are the ongoing source of our thankfulness. As Bo Giertz writes:

> Thankfulness and devotion to Him who died for us and reconciled us with God become the driving forces in our lives. He died for me. Consequently, I have died. My sin was also there on Golgotha. My old Adam with all its godlessness received its death sentence there. But He took that sentence upon Himself. Now I can live with Him and for Him. Now every day is a day of salvation and a time of pleasure, when His mercy surrounds me and carries me once again, and when He has duties for me once again that I can do in His service.[7]

O Lord, fill our hearts with thankfulness at all times! O Lord, help us give thanks to you in works that please you!

"Rise and go! Your faith has made you well!" What powerful words! They are words that urge the thankfulness spoken by the Samaritan to change into actions of thankfulness displayed in daily living. At the same time, Jesus gives the Samaritan another reason for thankfulness. The gift of faith! God had planted faith in this man's heart. Faith is not something we accomplish—it is something only God can give by the Holy Spirit working through the gospel. Cherish this gift of faith God has given you! Thank God for this gift. Nourish and care for this faith by going back to the gospel daily. God loves you! God forgives you! To this we can only utter in complete amazement. Thank you, Lord!

Lord, you have raised me up
To joy and exultation
And clearly shown the way
That leads to my salvation.
My sins are washed away;
For this I thank you, Lord.
Now with my heart and soul
All evil I abhor.

Grant that your Spirit's help
To me be always given
Lest I should fall again
And lose the way to heaven.
Grant that he give me strength
In my infirmity;
May he renew my heart
To serve you willingly.[8]

YOU ARE FORGIVEN—
TREASURE IT!

He who conceals his sins does not prosper, but whoever
confesses and renounces them finds mercy. (Proverbs 28:13)

"LORD, I AM BROKEN. Please fix me!" Those were the
very first words that began my journey of repentance. At
the time I was concealing my sins. It was not a prosperous time
for me. But God answered my prayer. The first part of fixing my
brokenness was to lead me to confess and renounce my sins. Over
time God led me to do just that. In so doing, I found mercy. It was
a mercy I had already known. It was a mercy I had the privilege
to proclaim to God's people every day. Now it was a mercy that
I appreciated in greater depth than ever before. The sinful nature
in me insisted that I was ruined. That sinful nature also insisted
that I had to do things to get back in God's favor. The reality is
that Christ has done it all. My sins are paid for in full, washed
away by the blood of Christ. God has forgiven me. My family
and friends have forgiven me. I have forgiven me. I am forgiven!
I know this with absolute certainty because God has assured me
of this fact over and over again in his word, through my pastors,
and through my family and friends. In addition, I am assured of
God's forgiveness as I recall my baptism and as I receive the Lord's

Supper. God has indeed answered my prayer! He continues to heal me through his gracious forgiveness.

God does the very same for you. Find comfort and joy as God reminds you of your forgiveness in Christ. Consider Peter. He denied knowing Christ. He sinned. He repented. Christ forgave him. Yes, Peter heard Jesus say to him, "Feed my sheep." Peter was privileged to share the good news of forgiveness with many others. You have the very same privilege. Show the world you are forgiven! Tell the world they are forgiven! Yes, you have received this great treasure from God. He has forgiven you. He has opened the doors of heaven to you. He has also given you his gospel to share with everyone you know.

Treasure your forgiveness with confidence! Doubt is the devil's device. He comes slithering into your life and whispers, "Did God really say?" The devil wants you to doubt. God gives the gift of confidence. After all, God is the one who planned, participated in, and purchased your forgiveness. God is the one who called you to faith in Jesus. God is the one who spoke to you through his Word and convinced you that he has forgiven you. God wants you to be confident to the point of boasting in him. We know that pride is a sin that leads us into all sorts of trouble. The devil wants us to be confident in ourselves and boastful about our deeds. If he cannot get us to be puffed up with pride, then the devil leads us to the pit of despair. Neither is a place where our gracious God wants us. Rather, our Lord would have us place all of our confidence in him. Our Savior would have us boast in him. The truth is he has saved us! In response to his great gift of salvation, we remain confident in him and boast in him. We take to heart the words of Romans 8:

> Therefore, there is now no condemnation for those who are in Christ Jesus ... For I am

convinced that neither death nor life, neither angels nor demons, neither the present nor the future, nor any powers, neither height nor depth, nor anything else in all creation, will be able to separate us from the love of God that is in Christ Jesus our Lord.

We listen to Paul's words to Timothy with rapt attention: Here is a trustworthy saying that deserves full acceptance: Christ Jesus came into the world to save sinners – of whom I am the worst.

Finally we also boldly pray with Paul, "May I never boast except in the cross of our Lord Jesus Christ, through which the world has been crucified to me, and I to the world." Christ has done all for us, and so the only thing we have to boast about is Christ and his forgiving work on our behalf. Our confidence is and remains in Jesus, for he has forgiven us!

Sounds easy! It even looks easy on paper. Jesus has done it all. Just keep confident in him. The trouble is our confidence or faith is constantly under attack. Satan keeps coming back to accuse me of my sin. The world calls on me in so many subtle ways to forget about Jesus. My own sinful flesh urges me to despair, give up, and remain uncertain. There is so much doubt swirling around me each day that it is difficult to remain confident. So I cry out to Jesus, echoing the words of the father who brought his demon possessed boy to Jesus: "I do believe; help me overcome my unbelief!" (Mark 9:24). Jesus drove the demon out of the man's boy. In the same way Jesus drives the doubt out of my heart. Daily I need to hear my Lord Jesus say, "Your sins are forgiven!" Daily Jesus forgives me. Jesus does the same for you. So daily return to scripture and find this comfort:

> The Lord is compassionate and gracious, slow
> to anger, abounding in love. He will not always
> accuse, nor will he harbor his anger forever; he
> does not treat us as our sins deserve or repay us
> according to our iniquities. For as high as the
> heavens are above the earth, so great is his love
> for those who fear him; as far as the east is from
> the west, so far has he removed our transgressions
> from us. (Psalm 103:8–12)

Daily doses of God's Word keep faith alive and help us overcome our unbelief. Jesus forgives our doubts. Jesus makes us certain that he has saved us.

Treasure your forgiveness with joy! This is the best joy possible. After one has fallen into sin and Satan has pulled you down to the depths of despair over your sin, there are no sweeter, more jubilant words to hear than that heavenly sentence, "Your sins are forgiven!" David knew this joy. He writes in Psalm 30, "You turned my wailing into dancing; you removed my sackcloth and clothed me with joy, that my heart may sing to you and not be silent. O Lord my God, I will give you thanks forever." Forgiven sin means you have a place in heaven. Jesus has taken all your sins away. This is the highest form of joy God gives—this joy of sin forgiven, this joy that your name is written in heaven. Yes, friends, we rejoice in the Lord. We rejoice that our sins are washed away in the blood of Jesus. We ask our God to keep us focused on him and his forgiveness, so we remain living in the joy that his forgiveness gives. We pray with the forgiven Psalmist, David: "Let me hear joy and gladness; let the bones you have crushed rejoice."

What does such joy look like? Does it mean I walk around with a smile on my face all the time? Does it mean I am never sad? Not at all! So how do I best describe the joy of living in God's love and forgiveness? I struggle to find the right words to describe the joy Jesus gives us. Let me share with you where I most often find such joy. I find this joy most often as I sit in the sanctuary at church in those quiet moments before worship begins or those moments of silent reflection at various points during worship. It is the moment of looking at the cross and recalling that is the symbol of my salvation. It was on a cross that Jesus purchased me. He paid my debt and made me free. But it does not end there. The baptismal font reminds me that in the waters of holy baptism God made me his own child. My sins are washed away. As I take in these sights, a calm confidence grows inside me. This is the joy God gives. It is the realization and the reminder of Lamentations 3: "Because of the Lord's great love we are not consumed, for his compassions are new every morning; great is your faithfulness." What does joy look like? It is not me jumping up and down for joy. It is me getting out of bed in the morning ready to enjoy the day the Lord has given me. This joy is not a constant feeling of elation. Rather it is a quiet certainty that God loves me and cares about me every second of every day. This joy allows me to face the setbacks, the failures, and the disappointments of daily life without concluding that God is punishing me for my sin. The focus of the joy God gives is on him, not on me. My moods change. Circumstances of life change. God's love for me never changes. This is the joy God gives. In this joy I know that God always loves me, and he will find a way to bless me that is far beyond anything I could ask or imagine.

Most often the biggest enemy of the joy God has bestowed on me in his grace and mercy is me. Certainly the devil does not want me to find joy in the Lord. Satan would prefer that I would revel in sin and disobedience. But when it comes to joy, I find that I am my own worst enemy. Maybe you have found this to be true in your life as well. The sinful nature likes to insist that we must be down in the dumps all the time because we are sinners. This is nothing more than a lack of trust in the Lord, for our God has clearly stated, "You are forgiven!" Our Lord Jesus paid the price for all of our sins, not just some of them. Our Lord Jesus completed the task of paying for sin. Jesus did not die for most of your sins. He died for all of them. Jesus did not do most of the job of winning your salvation. He did it all! Yes, Jesus declared from the cross, "It is finished!" His resurrection from the dead proves that God has accepted his payment for all sin. "He was delivered over to death for our sins and was raised to life for our justification" (Romans 4:25). So each day I need to go back to the cross and the empty tomb. Each day I need to be reminded that I am God's dearly loved, forgiven child. This remains the source of my joy even as I struggle to stay joyful and keep focused on the Lord. With Christians across the centuries, my spirits are lifted as I read the words of Psalm 100:

> Shout for joy to the Lord, all the earth. Serve the Lord with gladness; come before him with joyful songs. Know that the Lord is God. It is he who made us, and we are his; we are his people, the sheep of his pasture. Enter his gates with thanksgiving and his courts with praise; give thanks to him and praise his name. For the Lord is good and his love endures forever; his faithfulness continues through all generations.

Treasure your forgiveness with forgiveness! Allow me to take a moment to remind myself and you of this surprising fact that we are forgiven in Christ. The devil continues to work to cause us to doubt that Jesus died for me, that he forgives me. The devil lies to us and tells us that forgiveness does not apply to us, that somehow we did something so bad that it is not covered by the forgiveness Jesus won. The sinful flesh is quick to agree and begins to remind us of all the horrible things we have thought, said, and done. Friends, the fact remains that your sins—all of them—are forgiven!

At the time that Deb and I were beginning to talk after months of separation, we decided to go on a date. We were not sure how any of this would work. We were just trying to discover what forgiveness would look like for us and how we would rebuild our relationship. Because Deb had an obligation for work on Sunday morning, we decided to go to church Saturday evening before we went out for coffee. This was a decision that had a huge impact on our lives. That evening as we drove to church, our conversation turned to which pastor would be preaching. We both hoped that it would not be Pastor Panitzke. He was the pastor who had shepherded us individually through the horrible days after I confessed my sin. This was not because we did not appreciate his work. Rather we knew he would ask us how we were doing, and at this point neither of us had a clue how we were doing. Pastor Panitzke was the preacher that evening. He preached a sermon about Christ in Gethsemane under the theme, "Overwhelmed—for Me!" The sermon was fitting and the message comforting. But the most memorable thing about this sermon was the introduction. Pastor walked halfway down the center aisle at church.

He looked toward the entryway and began motioning, as if calling someone forward, and said, "Imagine for a moment that you are an Old Testament believer. You find yourself going to the temple with your family. Your father has insisted that you take the best lamb your family owns. This is a lamb you have cared for and have grown to love. When you arrive at the temple, the priest motions for your family to come forward. Your father takes the lamb to the priest. The priest lays his hand on the head of the lamb, grabs a knife, points to each member of your family, and says, 'Because you have sinned, this lamb must die.' After that the priest slits the throat of the lamb and watches its life blood drain out. The priest motions for the next family to come forward. They lead a goat up to the priest. The priest takes the goat, places his hand on its head, looks at each member of the family, and says, 'Because you have sinned, this goat must die.' Then the priest slits the throat of the goat. The priest motions for the next family to come forward. This family was poor and brought two doves. The priest takes the birds, points to each family member, and says, 'Because you have sinned, these birds must die.' The priest sacrifices the birds. Family after family brought their sacrifice to the priest and heard him say to them, 'Because you have sinned, this animal must die.' Now imagine you see Jesus as he is walking resolutely to his death on the cross." The preacher now pauses and motions for Jesus, then points to the whole congregation and says to us, "Because you have sinned, he must die."

Through this powerful imagery, the point became crystal clear because of my sin of adultery, Jesus must die. It is my guilt that caused his death. But his death was for my sin and to take away my guilt. My adultery is forgiven! All my sins are forgiven! Jesus did all he did for me and for my salvation. What amazing grace! Needless to say, Deb and I did not have dry eyes. We shed tears of joy to know Jesus secured forgiveness for us in his death and resurrection. On top of all that, we were able to receive the Lord's Supper together. This was an additional assurance of the forgiveness of sins. Certainly, this experience was emotionally draining and an excellent way to restart our journey through life together. After the service, no words were exchanged, and there were no questions of how we were doing. God's grace spoke volumes to us that evening. No matter what I had done, Jesus forgave me. So many other times I received assurance of forgiveness. Each time it is very much needed and appreciated. Forgiveness is not only a great gift from God of tremendous comfort, but it is also a beautiful way of life. God has forgiven me! This leads me to forgive those who sin against me.

We have observed that the devil lies to us as he tempts us to sin, that Satan accuses of sin and tries to convince us that God will not forgive us after we have sinned, and now we face another attack of our old evil foe. He tempts us to become unforgiving after we have received God's unconditional forgiveness. So we take to heart the warning of our Savior in his parable of the unforgiving servant.

> Then Peter came to Jesus and asked, "Lord, how many times shall I forgive my brother when he sins against me? Up to seven times?" Jesus answered, "I tell you, not seven times, but seventy-seven times." "Therefore, the kingdom of heaven is like a king who wanted to settle accounts with his servants. As he began the settlement, a man who owed him ten thousand talents was brought to him. Since he was not able to pay, the master ordered that he and his wife and his children and all that he had be sold to repay the debt. The servant fell on his knees before him. 'Be patient with me,' he begged, 'and I will pay back everything.' The servant's master took pity on him, canceled the debt and let him go. But when that servant went out, he found one of his fellow servants who owed him a hundred denarii. He grabbed him and began to choke him. 'Pay back what you owe me!' he demanded. His fellow servant fell to his knees and begged him, 'Be patient with me, and I will pay you back.' But he refused. Instead, he went off and had the man thrown into prison until he could pay the debt.

> When the other servants saw what had happened, they were greatly distressed and went and told their master everything that had happened. Then the master called the servant in. 'You wicked servant,' he said, 'I canceled all that debt of yours because you begged me to. Shouldn't you have had mercy on your fellow servant just as I had on you?' In anger his master turned him over to the jailers to be tortured, until he should pay back all he owed. This is how my heavenly Father will treat each of you unless you forgive each other from your heart." (Matthew 18:21-35).

This parable really needs no explanation. For those of us who have sinned and suffered through the guilt that follows sin, we pay very close attention. Remember the joy and elation you felt in your heart when you were fully convinced that God has forgiven you. Recall the comfort of knowing that Jesus paid your debt of sin to God in full on the cross and the Father marked that debt paid in full with the resurrection of Christ from the dead. Live in this forgiveness. Do not walk away from the good news that your sins are forgiven and go back to the old way of life without a thought. You are forgiven, so forgive!

Forgiveness cannot be demanded. Forgiveness is freely given. We receive Christ's forgiveness in one hand, and with the other we give forgiveness to our fellow sinner. The apostle Paul, who called himself the chief of sinners, puts it this way in Ephesians 4:32, "Be kind and compassionate to one another, forgiving each other, just as in Christ God forgave you." For me this is a mixed bag of sorts. I have a deeper appreciation than ever before in my life for God's forgiveness and the forgiveness graciously given to me by my wife, children, parents, family, church family, friends, and so on. At the same time, I can be filled with frustration with those who don't seem to want to forgive me. This is where the person who struggles with guilt may become angry. We know that God forgives. We know that our fellow Christians ought to forgive us as well. Some don't. How are we to treat them? At times we may want to scold them and tell them this parable. At times we may become angry with God that he doesn't seem to intervene. At times we avoid such folks altogether. In some cases we may hold a grudge and not forgive them for not forgiving us. If folks truly do not forgive us, that is to their spiritual peril, as evidenced by Jesus's parable. However, the same applies to us. So we forgive those who are unforgiving toward us from the heart. We know how God has treated us, and we strive, with God's help, to treat others in the very same way. Each time we forgive someone of their sins against us, we are reminded of how our God so graciously forgives us every day.

Allow me one more note regarding forgiveness. The scriptural concept of forgiveness is literally to send something away. What an amazing picture! Jesus takes our sin away—he picks it up and throws it away. What better thing could one do with sin but to throw it away like trash? This is precisely what our gracious God does for us. God says, "For I will forgive their wickedness and will remember their sins no more" (Jeremiah 31:34). God will send our sins away "as far as the east is from the west" (Psalm 103:12). God puts our sins out of sight and out of reach. "You have put all my sins behind your back (Isaiah 38:17). Also Micah 7:19: "You will again have compassion on us; you will tread our sins underfoot and hurl all our iniquities into the depths of the sea." Isaiah adds this comfort from the lips of God: "I, even I, am he who blots out your transgressions, for my own sake, and remembers your sins no more" (Isaiah 43:25). Again the Lord through Isaiah, "I have swept away your offenses like a cloud, your sins like the morning mist. Return to me, for I have redeemed you" (Isaiah 44:22). Yes, God has banished your sins and my sins. He has thrown them away! On top of that, God wants us to do the very same for those who sin against us. Why dwell on sin? No anger, no grudges—none of that! Throw those sins away just as God has!

Treasure your forgiveness with service! Jesus came down from heaven, took on human flesh, lived a perfect life in this imperfect world, went to battle against the Tempter in the wilderness, was arrested and accused unjustly, was beaten, crucified, died, and was buried. Jesus did all of that to serve me. Jesus did all of that to serve you. The story of my forgiveness is the story of Jesus serving me. The same holds true for you. In fact, I have learned in so many ways that humble service is the greatest thing in the world. It is humble service that has won our eternal salvation. It is also humble service that is our greatest privilege as a result of the forgiveness of sins.

We live to serve because Jesus lived to serve and save us. We clearly see this truth proclaimed in an account from Matthew 20:

> Then the mother of Zebedee's sons came to Jesus with her sons and, kneeling down, asked a favor of him. "What is it you want?" he asked. She said, "Grant that one of these two sons of mine may sit at your right and the other at your left in your kingdom." "You don't know what you are asking." Jesus said to them, "Can you drink the cup I am going to drink?" "We can," they answered. Jesus said to them, "You will indeed drink from my cup, but to sit at my right or left is not for me to grant. These places belong to those for whom they have been prepared by my Father." When the ten heard about this, they were indignant with the two brothers. Jesus called them together and

said, "You know that the rulers of the Gentiles
lord it over them, and their high officials exercise
authority over them. Not so with you. Instead,
whoever wants to become great among you must
be your servant, and whoever wants to be first
must be your slave—just as the Son of Man did
not come to be served, but to serve, and to give
his life as a ransom for many."

Here we come to the heart of Christianity. What no one else
could do for us, what we could not do for ourselves, Jesus did for
us—he gave himself as a ransom for us. This is not an accident,
and this is not an incident. This is the one purpose of Jesus—he
came to give his life as a ransom for many. His free life is given in
exchange for our forfeited life. The worth of his life outweighs the
sin of the world. God in his grace brings us to accept this ransom
by his gift of faith, so we become Christians. We prove ourselves
Christians by showing the spirit of Christ. Jesus came not to be
served but to serve others; so we are Christians for the purpose
not of being served, but to serve others. This is far from the pride
that leads us to sin and eternal destruction. This is humbly serving
Christ who served us. This is serving others because Christ has
served us.

Jesus has set me free from sinful selfishness and pride. Jesus has
set me free from sin and guilt. Jesus has set me free to serve.
Paul writes in Galatians 5:13, "You, my brothers, were called
to be free. But do not use your freedom to indulge the sinful
nature; rather, serve one another in love." I am free to serve. So
I am happy to serve in my home as I serve my wife, children,
parents, and extended family. I am happy to serve my employer.
I am happy to serve my brothers and sisters in Christ in my
congregation. I also pray that God would use me to serve those
who are suffering through sin and its consequences, those who

struggle with guilt. The purpose of this book is to reach out to you who are suffering from guilt and shame. I humbly pray that I can in some small way serve you. Christian living is not about pride and position. Christian living is about humble service. In fact, a great way to stay away from pride that leads to our spiritual destruction is to go about the work of service.

So often over the years that it has taken to write this account, I have wanted to shy away from serving in our congregation. It seems so much easier not to have to answer the questions about why I had to resign from public ministry. It seems so much easier to sit back and enjoy being served with the gospel. Two things prevented me from sitting on the sidelines. First, Christ's love kept on compelling me to serve. Second, Deb encouraged me to use the gifts I have in service to others. She said while it is difficult to serve at times, we simply could not stop serving. So we have served in a number of ways when asked. It is still difficult not to have the privilege of teaching and preaching. I truly miss it. At the same time, it is such a great gift to serve in any small way. Serving is a way of life for Christians because of the great service Christ has performed for us.

ACCUSED—CONDEMNED—
ACQUITTED—COMPELLED

S O THIS IS MY story of sin, guilt, and shame. But it is also the story of God answering the prayer of a sinful man who had just begun to wrestle with guilt. The prayer was short and pointed: "Lord, fix me." Am I completely fixed? No. That doesn't come until the day I enter the eternal rest of heaven. Am I completely forgiven? Absolutely!

God's law accused and condemned me for my sin. This was indeed an act of God's love, for God used his law not only to show me my sins but also to show me my deep need for a Savior. No matter what I did, I could not work my way out of sin and guilt. I could not save myself. Only Jesus could do that.

From what you have read so far, you may have the impression that guilt and shame are always bad. That is not the case at all. Guilt and shame are rather neutral things. God always uses these things correctly and for our good. Satan uses these things to torment us and to separate us from God.

Perhaps a story to illustrate the way guilt works will help. Years ago I was training our golden retriever for duck hunting. The dog did a fantastic job of taking a straight line to the retrieve. However, once she picked up the bird, she would not come straight back.

Rather she would wander around with the bird until she felt like she was done playing. It was extremely important to correct this behavior. Why? Because at some point she would be required to retrieve a bird in the rough and icy waters of November. Then it would be important to go straight to the downed bird, pick it up, and come straight back, limiting exposure to the cold water and keeping the dog safe. In order to correct this behavior, I used a thirty-foot-long cord attached to her collar. When she began to wander off course, one tug on the cord would keep her from wandering and bring her straight back. After the lesson was learned, the cord was no longer needed. If the wrong behavior started coming back, then the cord would come back, and we would relearn the lesson. You can see the importance of the cord training to the safety and well-being of the dog. At the same time, if one just used the cord to constantly torment the dog, you would no longer call it training but abuse. God uses guilt to make us aware we are sinning and to drive us to seek his help. God uses guilt like I used the cord with the dog—to serve a good purpose. Satan uses guilt in an abusive way just to torment us. Guilt used to drive us to despair of ourselves and to turn to Jesus, for his mercy is good. Guilt used to drive us to despair and keep us there is evil.

God's gospel announced the good news that I am acquitted of all wrongdoing because Jesus was punished in my place. What great comfort and joy this brings to life. No matter what, God loves me! No matter what, Jesus has won my forgiveness! It is this forgiveness that compels me to service!

This is the pattern of life for Christians: accused—condemned—acquitted—compelled. It is something we do over and over again. In fact, every day we look into the mirror of God's law and see where we have offended him. We review the Ten Commandments and see how we have failed. We are accused and condemned. But our daily spiritual exercise does not stop there. We also daily

hear the words of promise that all is forgiven in Christ. We stand
acquitted before God, not guilty of any sin because of Jesus Christ.
This is what compels us to flee from sin and live by God's direction.

> Chief of sinners though I be,
> Jesus shed his blood for me,
> Died that I might live on high,
> Lives that I might never die.
> As a branch is to the vine,
> I am his and he is mine!
>
> Only Jesus can impart
> Comfort to a wounded heart;
> Peace that flows from sin forgiven,
> Joy that lifts the soul to heaven,
> Faith and hope to walk with God
> In the way that Enoch trod.
>
> Strengthen me, O gracious Lord,
> By your Spirit and your word.
> When my wayward heart would stray,
> Keep me in the narrow way;
> Grace in time of need supply
> While I live and when I die.[9]

THE SAMARITAN
WAY OF LIFE

"I T AIN'T ALL ABOUT you, child!" That is what the mother said to her crying daughter in the museum gift shop. The little girl was acting up because she wanted a toy that the mom was not buying. So the temper tantrum began. In a remarkable way, this mother brought the entire situation into focus. What a life lesson that girl and the rest of us within earshot learned that day! So true. It is not all about me. It is not all about you. Life is so much more than an obsession with self. This is the lesson of the Samaritan.

This lesson was brought home in a very personal way. As the work of writing this account drew to a close, I made a request to my church body to return to public ministry. The initial e-mail never received a reply. Very little information was offered when I inquired. It was a very frustrating time. Finally, after two more e-mails and a face-to-face request, the news arrived! It was not the news for which I hoped and prayed. On the basis of 1 Timothy 3:2 ("Now the overseer must be above reproach, the husband of but one wife") the request was denied. So it was stated, "We believe, on the basis of 1 Timothy 3:2 and Titus 1:6, those actions (committing adultery) disqualified you from public ministry and still disqualify you. Because of those actions, you are no longer blameless and above reproach. We acknowledge that you have but one wife and she is the wife with whom you were joined in marriage years ago, but you are no longer a one-woman man like the man who married and has been faithful to his marriage vows."

I am the Samaritan. My sin causes people to look down on me, to ridicule me, to exclude me. I am unable to return to the same form of service I once enjoyed. In all of this turmoil, it is easy to become discouraged and give up. I am the Samaritan, and Jesus still loves me! This is all that matters. It is all about Jesus!

The Samaritan is that person who is looked down upon, the sinner, the one who has made a mess of things. The Samaritan is the lost person. Jesus is the one who comes in search of the lost. Jesus is the Good Shepherd who leaves the ninety-nine sheep behind to search for the one lost sheep. Jesus has done that for you. Jesus has done that for me. Therein is the secret of life. It is all about Christ!

So join me in leaving sin, guilt, and shame behind! Join me in living in faith and love. Faith is from Christ and is focused on Christ. Faith receives the good from God. Love is from Christ and imitates Christ. Love gives the good to our neighbor.

Join me in fighting the daily battle against sin, self, and Satan. Life in this sinful world is a struggle. But Jesus is always with us. He comforts us as he says, "In this world you will have trouble. But take heart! I have overcome the world" (John 16:33).

The Samaritan way of life shares the good news of Jesus with our village, takes the time to help those in need, and is always mindful that all we have is from our gracious God. The Samaritan way of life rejoices that sin is forgiven, forgives those who sin against us, and is always thankful for the love God shows us in Christ. The Samaritan way of life does not dwell on self-pity. Nor does it hold grudges. Through hard times and great prosperity, it focuses on Christ alone!

Dear fellow Samaritan, I pray this account helps you see God's love for you. While this story is my story and an account about me, I hope you see the bigger story. It is the story of God's merciful love to sinners. It is a story meant to share God's love with you. In the end, this story is about God. May He bless you through this account and bring you the peace of knowing His love for you!

> To him who is able to keep you from falling
> and to present you before his glorious presence
> without fault and with great joy—to the only God
> our Savior be glory, majesty, power and authority,
> through Jesus Christ our Lord, before all ages,
> now and forevermore! Amen. (Jude 24–25)[10]

ENDNOTES

1   This is the account from Mark 14. See also Matthew 26 and Luke 22.

2   Gary and Mona Shriver, *Unfaithful: Hope and Healing After Infidelity* (Colorado Springs, CO: David C. Cook, 2009).

3   www.hopeandhealing.us

4   From the hymn, "Stricken, Smitten, and Afflicted" by Thomas Kelly.

5   From the hymn, "Jesus Paid It All" by Elvina M. Hall.

6   *Sermons of Martin Luther,* edited by John Nicholas Lenker. Volume 5 Sermons on Gospel Texts for the 13th to 26th Sundays after Trinity (Grand Rapids, MI: Baker Book House, 1988), 30.

7   Bo Giertz, translated by Richard Wood with Bror Erickson, *To Live With Christ* (St. Louis, MO: Concordia Publishing House, 2008) 775.

8   From the hymn, "How Can I Thank You, Lord" by David Denicke.

[9]   From the hymn, "Chief of Sinners Though I Be" by William McComb.

[10] All Scripture quotations are taken from the Holy Bible, New International Version, NIV. Copyright 1973, 1978, 1984 by International Bible Society.

If you need additional help with guilt and shame or you have additional questions, contact that author at Samaritan4given@gmail.com.

Printed in the United States
By Bookmasters